THE
FRIENDLY
PRAIRIE
DOG

THE FRIENDLY

PRAIRIE DOG

Denise Casey

Illustrated with color photographs
by Dr. Tim W. Clark and others

DODD, MEAD & COMPANY   New York

To Erin, Levi, Wyatt, and Heath

PHOTOGRAPH CREDITS

Franz J. Camenzind, page 1, 22-23, 33; J. Perley
Fitzgerald, 29, 34-35 (bottom); Louise Richardson
Forrest, 7 (bottom), 8 (top), and 17. All other
photographs are by Dr. Tim W. Clark.

Distributed in Canada by
McClelland and Stewart Limited, Toronto
Printed in Hong Kong by South China Printing Company
Designed by Jean Krulis

1 2 3 4 5 6 7 8 9 10

Library of Congress Cataloging-in-Publication Data

Casey, Denise.
The friendly prairie dog.

Includes index.
Summary: Simple text and photographs introduce the physical
characteristics, habits, and natural environment of the
prairie dog, a cousin of the squirrel.
1. Prairie dogs—Juvenile literature.   [1. Prairie dogs]   I. Title.
QL737.R68C36   1987   599.32′32   86-23932
ISBN 0-396-08901-1

PLUMP PRAIRIE DOGS

Prairie dogs are plump rodents, cousins of the squirrels. They are about one foot tall and weigh one to three pounds.

5

Their legs are so short that
their bellies may rub the
ground.

Short black or white tails
flicker and wag all day.

Strong teeth clip and grind green plants. Long, sharp claws are for digging.

Prairie dogs are lively, alert animals, with keen eyesight and hearing.

8

BURROWS AND TOWNS

Prairie dogs dig underground tunnels to live in. These burrows stay warm in winter and cool in summer. They have cozy, dry rooms with soft, grass-lined nests. The dirt mounds around the entrances make good lookout posts.

Prairie dogs live together in groups, called towns, on the grassy plains of western North America.

Many harmless neighbors share the towns with the prairie dogs, including rabbits, pronghorns, and bison.

But some animals live near the towns to hunt the prairie dogs— eagles, snakes, coyotes, and black-footed ferrets, for instance.

When frightened, the prairie dogs
dive headfirst into the safety of their
burrows.

DAILY LIFE

"*Wee-oo! Wee-oo!*" A big tan prairie dog leaps into the air, throws back his head and paws, and sings "*Wee-oo!*" This seems to mean that all is safe.

As the sun comes up, sleepy prairie dogs crawl from their burrows to bask in the warm sunshine.

They greet their family and neighbors with a "kiss," rubbing noses and teeth together.

They waddle along looking
for plants to eat.

Prairie dogs clean their burrows by scratching the soil and patting the dirt around the mounds with their noses.

Grasses are carried underground to make nests for young and adults.

Each family of one father, several
mothers, and their pups has its own
territory within the town and may
fight to defend it.

A NEIGHBORLY COMMUNITY

Prairie dogs are very sociable animals. Neighbors gather together for grooming. They scratch through one another's fur to clean it.

Prairie dogs keep in touch by barking, "*Yek-yek-yek*." They chatter and chirp and growl. Each one watches for dangers and quickly alerts the whole town with a warning bark, "*Chirk*."

They also signal with a wag or flick of their tails.

Some animals, such as lizards, hawks, and weasels, live alone. But prairie dogs need to live together and communicate. This is as important to them as food and burrows.

GROWING UP

Litters of four to six babies are born underground in the spring. At birth, they are tiny and helpless. Their mothers care for them and provide milk. The fathers live nearby, but do not help raise the pups.

When they are about six weeks old,
the young climb up to explore their
town for the first time.

They play chasing
and wrestling
games.

The pups grow fast. By fall, they are almost full grown. They learn which plants to eat and which animals to hide from. They learn the meanings of *"chirk,"* *"wee-oo,"* and *"yek-yek-yek."*

EATING

The prairie dogs' biggest job all summer is to eat and get fat.

They munch weeds and seeds and grass; they dig roots and catch bugs.

Nibble, nibble, nibble.

Fat helps them survive the long
winter when they sleep a lot and eat
little, since snow covers the plants
they eat.

PRAIRIE DOGS AND PEOPLE

Some parks and zoos have prairie dog towns that people can watch up close. These prairie dogs are used to people and are not afraid.

Some ranchers don't like prairie dogs. They believe that prairie dogs eat the grass needed for cattle and sheep. And if farmers plant crops on a prairie dog town, the prairie dogs will eat the crops.

But prairie dogs are an important part of the prairie. Their digging helps make new soil, and they are good neighbors to many other animals.

INDEX